NEW YEAR NEW YOU

How To Make Every Year Your Year

By

KENNETH BARNES

CONTENTS

INTRODUCTION _________________________ 5

DEVELOPING PERSONAL CONFIDENCE _____ 11

ENERGY AND STAMINA _______________ 19

THE POWER OF ASSOCIATION ___________ 27

HABITS OF THE SUCCESSFUL_______________ 33

CONCLUSION_________________________ 37

INTRODUCTION

My name is Kenneth Barnes, and I was born and raised in New Orleans

I want to share a little bit about who I am before delving into my thoughts and advice. My goal with this book is to bring value to you which can be implemented immediately into your day-to-day grind and begin to see an impact.

I have traveled over the years for business, both domestically and internationally, and whenever I tell people I'm from New Orleans, they almost always have a story or experience of the city.

Most of the time they know about Mardi Gras, beignets, bourbon, and St. Charles, where the street car runs. And even though I know those areas and love them, my experience growing up 5 blocks off of St. Charles was like living in a different world.

One had maids and butlers, the other had crackheads, thefts, and even sometimes, shootings.

Growing up poor was incredibly frustrating, my parents sacrificed to send me to private school, which I'm grateful for, but it really taught me how poor we and others in our neighborhood were.

It was my private school experience that actually showed me how different people lived from myself, especially when there were Freshmen in high school driving BMWs and Mercedes-Benzes, while my parents couldn't afford those things.

As a kid, this had me very confused and extremely frustrated.

Frustrated because my grandfather was a Pastor, so we spent a lot of time in Church, but were still not financially free.

It made me ask questions like, does God love everyone the same? If so, shouldn't we all start off with the same amount of money, as in the game of Monopoly?

The only thing I knew for sure was poverty sucked and I wanted out. I wanted to have the Jordans that my parents couldn't afford or really anything extra besides our needs, a home, food on the table, and an education.

I remember trying to get jobs like gathering the buggies at Winn Dixie but was told I didn't have any work experience...I was like, how will I get work experience if no one gives me a shot? This desire to make money eventually led me to ask a neighborhood drug dealer for an opportunity to work with him.

He and his friends had nice cars, the girls, and I saw a way for me to get the things I desired.

This is why I understand fully how tough it is to come from nothing and the only real routes for getting out were to play ball, rap, or sell drugs.

There were no examples of really becoming the CEO of JP Morgan. It's a survival of the fittest and the large majority don't make it out.

I was extremely fortunate to make it out due to a good friend of mine growing up, who also got into the drug game and grew significantly in the game. He saw that I came from a good family and really had a chance to make it out, and told me about a job at the company his sister worked. They were hiring representatives to sell beepers and cell phones.

This opportunity introduced me to corporate America and taught me that there were other ways to work hard and change your financial situation legally.

There were still missing pieces because a lot of people work hard every day, but yet still struggle financially in their lives.

And this made me curious to find out why ....what was the difference...what were the reasons some people are successful and others are not?

I also knew from being observant and studying information, that it wasn't based on gender or race, because in every city, state, and country, there are the rich and the poor.

I made it my mission to find out why, and what things made the difference between these two financial levels.

This book will give you the introductory principles to become aware of the differences and begin to explore the journey. Sometimes we are even our greatest enemy - an important reason why we often do not succeed.

Even very successful people know failure, and defeat, and have made mistakes. Oftentimes, great successes have been paid for with long dry spells and great failures. Ray Kroc (52), the founder of the McDonald's Corporation, persuaded the McDonald brothers, Richard and Maurice, to give him the franchise rights and the McDonald's name in return for a 0.5 percent share in sales. Then he went through various crises and bankruptcies with his company for six years before everything worked out.

It is always exciting to collect the different meanings each person has for "success" on a flipchart in a seminar group.

Ten participants, at least 20 different meanings and ideas about success. For me, success is when something is successful. Some people wait their entire lives for success and for paradise or happiness to fall into their laps, and it just doesn't. This idea of how success works, as shown on film and television, does not coincide with how reality truly is.

Life always has ups and downs on the way to our goals and visions. The question is, where do we learn the most? Exactly, in the valleys and swamps of life.

It is also very important that when you write down your vision, you do not follow, copy, or imitate others, but that you take the time to write down your vision, what inspires you, and what you really think about yourself and your life that you want to achieve.

You need to explore what you're really passionate about.

DEVELOPING PERSONAL CONFIDENCE

A key component of the process of making every year your best year is developing your self-confidence. Not only is confidence a quality, but it's also an attitude that can be developed and reinforced with practice. We'll use lessons from "The Confident Mind" in this chapter to help you build unwavering confidence in so many areas of your life.

1. Self-awareness:

Being self-aware is the first step towards developing confidence. It entails having a thorough awareness of your advantages and disadvantages. No matter how minor your accomplishments may seem, take some time to consider them. Rewarding yourself for accomplishments, no matter how small, helps you feel good about yourself. The groundwork for focused attempts at personal development is laid by this insight.

When you recognize your strengths, you can leverage them to tackle challenges with assurance. Conversely, understanding your weaknesses is not a cause for self-doubt but an opportunity for growth. The journey toward confidence often involves turning weaknesses into areas of improvement. As you embrace self-awareness, you gain clarity about who you are and what you bring to the table, fostering a sense of authenticity that radiates confidence.

2. Positive self-talk:

The language we use internally has a profound impact on our confidence. Positive self-talk involves consciously replacing negative thoughts with affirmations that uplift and empower. Instead of dwelling on perceived failures or shortcomings, intentionally focus on your achievements and capabilities. Challenge and reframe negative beliefs about yourself by questioning their validity and replacing them with positive, constructive alternatives.

Positive self-talk is not about denying challenges or difficulties; rather, it's a shift in perspective that allows you to approach setbacks as opportunities for learning and growth. By cultivating a habit of constructive self-dialogue, you create a mental environment that supports confidence and resilience.

3. Set realistic goals:

Confidence flourishes in the soil of achievement. Setting realistic goals is a practical strategy to incrementally build confidence. Break down larger goals into smaller, manageable steps. This not only makes the objectives more achievable but also provides a series of victories that contribute to a sense of accomplishment.

Celebrating small victories is crucial in this process. Whether it's completing a task ahead of schedule, mastering a new skill, or overcoming a challenge, each success contributes to a growing reservoir of confidence. By recognizing and appreciating your progress, you reinforce the belief that you can overcome obstacles and achieve your objectives.

4. Preparation and practice:

Confidence is closely tied to competence. Thorough preparation for tasks or challenges is a tangible way to enhance confidence. Whether it's a presentation, job interview, or a new skill, invest time and effort in getting ready. This preparation not only boosts your knowledge and skills but also provides a sense of control over the situation.

Practice is another essential element in building confidence. Repeatedly engaging in activities that challenge you gradually diminishes anxiety and reinforces competence. As you become more proficient through practice, the unfamiliar transforms into the familiar, fostering confidence in your abilities.

5. Body language:

Non-verbal communication is a powerful aspect of confidence. Your body language often speaks louder than words. Maintain good posture, stand tall, and adopt open gestures. Projecting confidence through your body language not only influences how others perceive you but also impacts your internal mindset.

Making eye contact is a simple yet effective way to convey confidence. It establishes a connection with others and communicates a sense of self-assuredness. Additionally, using purposeful gestures can emphasize your points and convey confidence in your communication.

6. Learn from failures:

Failure is not the opposite of confidence; it's a stepping stone to success. Viewing failures as opportunities for growth is a transformative mindset. When faced with setbacks, take the time to analyze what went wrong and identify lessons learned. This reflective approach turns failures into valuable experiences that contribute to your personal and professional development.

Understanding that failure is a natural part of any journey helps destigmatize setbacks. Embracing a mindset that values the lessons embedded in failure fosters resilience and fortifies your confidence in facing future challenges.

7. Accept compliments graciously:

Confident individuals know how to accept compliments graciously. Instead of deflecting praise or downplaying your achievements, practice saying "thank you" with sincerity. Accepting compliments with grace not only acknowledges your efforts but also reinforces positive feedback, contributing to a more positive self-image.

Learning to receive compliments is not about arrogance but about recognizing and internalizing positive feedback. It aligns with the idea that your accomplishments are worthy of acknowledgment and appreciation.

8. Surround yourself with positive influences:

Confidence is often influenced by the company you keep. Building a supportive network of friends and mentors can provide encouragement and constructive feedback. Surround yourself with people who uplift you, believe in your abilities, and offer guidance when needed.

Conversely, limit exposure to negative influences that may undermine your confidence. Toxic relationships or environments can erode self-esteem. By cultivating a positive support system, you create a nurturing environment that fosters confidence and personal growth.

9. Continuous learning:

Confidence is not a static state but a dynamic attribute that evolves through continuous learning. Stay curious and embrace new challenges as opportunities for growth. Acquiring new skills and knowledge not only enhances your competence but also expands your comfort zone.

Approach learning with a growth mindset, recognizing that your abilities can be developed through dedication and hard work. Embracing a mentality of continuous improvement contributes to a sense of self-efficacy and confidence in your ability to adapt and thrive in various situations.

10. Visualization:

Visualization is a powerful technique used by many confident individuals. By mentally picturing yourself succeeding in different situations, you create a positive mental image. Visualization taps into the power of the subconscious mind, influencing your beliefs and behaviors.

Take time to visualize successful outcomes before engaging in challenging activities. Whether it's a presentation, a meeting, or a performance, mentally rehearse the steps and imagine yourself confidently navigating the situation. Visualization serves as a powerful tool to align your thoughts with the confident version of yourself.

11. Mindfulness and relaxation techniques:

Confidence is closely linked to a calm and focused state of mind. Practice mindfulness to stay present and centered. Mindfulness involves paying attention to the present moment without judgment. By cultivating mindfulness, you can reduce anxiety and maintain composure in challenging situations.

Incorporate relaxation techniques, such as deep breathing or progressive muscle relaxation, into your routine. These practices help manage stress and promote a sense of calm, creating a conducive mental environment for confidence to thrive.

12. Celebrate progress:

Amidst the pursuit of larger goals, it's essential to celebrate the journey and acknowledge your progress. Regularly review and appreciate your achievements, no matter how small. Recognizing your growth instills a sense of pride and reinforces the belief that you are capable of overcoming challenges.

Celebrate not only the destination but also the milestones along the way. This positive reinforcement contributes to a self-perpetuating cycle of confidence, where each success builds upon the last, propelling you toward greater accomplishments.

Developing personal confidence is a multi-faceted journey that involves self-awareness, positive self-talk, goal-setting, preparation, and continuous learning. By integrating these principles into your mindset and behavior, you can cultivate a strong sense of confidence that empowers you to navigate life's challenges with assurance and resilience.

ENERGY AND STAMINA

Energy and stamina are critical components of overall well-being, and they are influenced by various factors including health, nutrition, and physical conditioning. Let's delve into each of these aspects and understand how they contribute to sustaining energy levels and building stamina in our daily lives.

Understanding the Body's Energy Systems

To comprehend how to optimize energy, it's essential to understand the body's energy systems. We'll explore the principles outlined by experts in the field, shedding light on how nutrition, exercise, and rest contribute to a harmonious and sustainable energy balance.

Health:

1. Regular Health Check-ups:

Regular health check-ups serve as a proactive measure in maintaining optimal energy levels and stamina. These check-ups can detect and address any underlying health issues that may be sapping your vitality. Conditions such as anemia, thyroid problems, or chronic illnesses can significantly impact energy levels. Timely intervention and treatment can not only alleviate symptoms but also restore and enhance your overall well-being.

2. Adequate Sleep:

The foundation of good health and sustained energy lies in the realm of quality sleep. Lack of sleep can lead to fatigue, diminished cognitive function, and a general sense of lethargy. Establishing a consistent sleep routine and ensuring a comfortable sleep environment are essential practices. Quality sleep not only rejuvenates the body but also plays a crucial role in mental and emotional resilience, reinforcing your capacity to face daily challenges with vitality.

3. Stress Management:

Chronic stress can be a silent energy thief, sapping your stamina and affecting both mental and physical health. Implementing effective stress management techniques is paramount. Practices such as mindfulness, meditation, or yoga can help create a balance between mental and physical well-being. By addressing stressors and learning to manage them effectively, you not only preserve your energy but also cultivate a resilient mindset that enhances overall stamina.

Nutrition:

1. Balanced Diet:

Nutrition is a cornerstone of sustained energy and stamina. Consuming a well-balanced diet ensures that your body receives the necessary nutrients for optimal functioning. Include a mix of carbohydrates, proteins, healthy fats, vitamins, and minerals in your meals. Carbohydrates provide a steady release of energy, proteins support muscle health, and fats contribute to overall satiety and sustained energy.

2. Hydration:

Dehydration can lead to fatigue, reduced cognitive function, and decreased physical performance. Adequate hydration is vital for maintaining energy levels and stamina. Ensure regular water intake throughout the day, and consider incorporating electrolyte-rich beverages, especially during physical activities or in warm climates. Proper hydration supports various bodily functions, from digestion to temperature regulation, contributing to overall vitality.

3. Regular Meals:

Eating regular, smaller meals throughout the day helps in maintaining stable blood sugar levels. This prevents the energy crashes associated with large, infrequent meals. Choosing nutrient-dense foods and incorporating a variety of fruits, vegetables, lean proteins, and whole grains provides a sustained source of energy. This dietary approach not only fuels your body but also supports overall health and well-being.

4. Limiting Caffeine and Sugar:

While caffeine can provide a temporary energy boost, excessive consumption can lead to energy crashes and disrupt sleep patterns. Similarly, refined sugars can cause spikes and crashes in blood sugar levels. Opt for moderate caffeine intake and consider alternatives like herbal teas. Choose complex carbohydrates and natural sugars from fruits and whole foods for more sustained energy without the rollercoaster effect on your energy levels.

Physical Conditioning:

1. Regular Exercise:

Physical conditioning is a key pillar in building and maintaining stamina. Regular exercise contributes to cardiovascular health, muscular strength, and overall fitness. Cardiovascular exercises, such as running or cycling, enhance endurance, while strength training builds muscular resilience. Flexibility exercises contribute to joint health and overall agility. Engaging in a well-rounded exercise routine not only boosts physical stamina but also has positive effects on mental well-being.

2. Gradual Progression:

When embarking on a new exercise routine or modifying an existing one, a gradual progression is crucial. This allows the body to adapt to increasing demands, reducing the risk of injuries and preventing excessive fatigue. Sudden, intense workouts can lead to burnout and decrease stamina. A gradual and consistent approach to physical conditioning ensures sustainable progress and long-term benefits.

3. Rest and Recovery:

Adequate rest and recovery are integral parts of any effective physical conditioning program. Overtraining can lead to burnout, increased susceptibility to injuries, and decreased stamina. Incorporate rest days into your routine and prioritize sufficient sleep for recovery. This allows the body to repair and strengthen, ensuring that you approach each workout with renewed energy and enthusiasm.

4. Consistency:

Consistency is the bedrock of building stamina through physical conditioning. Regular, moderate-intensity exercise over time enhances cardiovascular health, muscular strength, and endurance. Whether it's a daily walk, gym session, or team sports, maintaining consistency in your physical activity routine contributes to a sustained and cumulative improvement in stamina.

Lifestyle Factors:

1. Posture and Ergonomics:

Beyond diet and exercise, daily habits such as posture play a role in energy levels. Poor posture can lead to muscle fatigue and diminished energy. Maintaining good posture, especially for those with sedentary jobs, is crucial. Ergonomic adjustments to your workspace, such as an ergonomic chair and proper desk height, can prevent unnecessary strain on your body and maintain energy levels throughout the day.

2. Breaks and Movement:

Taking short breaks during prolonged periods of sitting or focused work can prevent mental and physical fatigue. Incorporate movements and stretches to keep the body active. Simple activities like standing up, stretching, or taking a short walk can refresh your mind and contribute to sustained energy levels. These breaks not only prevent monotony but also enhance overall productivity.

3. Limiting Sedentary Behavior:

Prolonged sitting is associated with decreased energy levels and negative health outcomes. Break up long periods of sitting with short walks, stretching exercises, or quick movement breaks. Incorporating movement into your daily routine not only boosts energy but also contributes to long-term health and well-being.

Mental Well-being:

1. Mind-Body Connection:

Mental well-being is intricately connected to physical stamina. Practices that enhance the mind-body connection, such as meditation, deep breathing, and mindfulness, contribute to overall energy and vitality. These practices promote a sense of calm, reduce stress, and foster mental clarity, all of which positively impact physical stamina.

2. Goal Setting:

Setting realistic and achievable goals provides a sense of purpose and motivation. Whether in the realm of fitness, career, or personal development, having clear goals creates a roadmap for action. Achieving these goals, whether they are short-term or long-term, provides a sense of accomplishment that boosts confidence and energy levels. Goal setting aligns your actions with your aspirations, creating a positive and purpose-driven mindset.

3. Positive Relationships:

Building and maintaining positive relationships contribute significantly to emotional well-being. Positive social connections provide emotional support, reduce stress, and contribute to an overall positive mindset. Healthy relationships create a sense of belonging and security, fostering mental and emotional resilience. The positive emotional state that arises from supportive relationships positively influences physical stamina and energy levels.

The intricate interplay between health, nutrition, physical conditioning, and lifestyle factors is central to the cultivation of daily energy and stamina. By recognizing and addressing each of these components, individuals can optimize their physical and mental well-being. It's not about isolated efforts but a holistic approach that integrates these elements into a cohesive lifestyle. Paying attention to health through regular check-ups, adopting a balanced and nutritious diet, engaging in regular physical activity, and prioritizing mental well-being collectively contribute to sustained energy levels and enhanced stamina. This holistic approach is an investment in long-term health and vitality, allowing individuals to navigate the challenges of daily life with resilience and vigor.

THE POWER
OF ASSOCIATION

In the pursuit of making every year your year, understanding the profound impact of the company you keep is paramount. The people we surround ourselves with play a pivotal role in shaping our perspectives, behaviors, and ultimately, the outcomes we experience in life.

The Dynamics of Influence:

The saying "You are the average of the five people you spend the most time with" holds a profound truth. Human beings are social creatures, and our interactions with others significantly impact our thoughts, emotions, and actions. The power of association lies in the dynamic exchange of energy, ideas, and values that occurs within our social circles.

Positive Influence:

Surrounding ourselves with positive influences can uplift and inspire us. Positive associations can provide support during challenging times, offer valuable insights, and motivate us to reach our full potential. Whether it's friends, mentors, or colleagues, those who exude positivity and encouragement contribute to a healthier mindset, fostering personal growth and resilience.

1. Motivation and Inspiration:

Positive associations often serve as a source of motivation and inspiration. Being around individuals who have achieved success or are actively pursuing their goals can ignite our aspirations. Their achievements become a testament to what is possible, encouraging us to aim higher and persevere in the face of challenges.

2. Shared Values:

Meaningful connections are often rooted in shared values. When we associate with those who align with our core principles, our actions and decisions become more congruent with our beliefs. This alignment creates a sense of harmony and purpose, leading to a more fulfilling and authentic life.

3. Emotional Support:

Positive associations provide a crucial support system during difficult times. Having a network of individuals who offer emotional support, understanding, and encouragement can make challenges more manageable. This emotional reinforcement bolsters our resilience and contributes to a more positive outlook.

Negative Influence:

Conversely, negative associations can have detrimental effects on various aspects of our lives. Toxic relationships, pessimistic attitudes, and unsupportive environments can hinder personal development and impede the pursuit of goals. Recognizing and addressing negative influences is essential for fostering a positive and constructive life.

1. Draining Energy:

Negative associations can drain our energy and enthusiasm. Constant exposure to pessimism, criticism, or toxicity can erode our motivation and hinder our ability to maintain a positive mindset. It's crucial to identify sources of negativity and set boundaries to protect our well-being.

2. Limiting Beliefs:

The beliefs and attitudes of those around us can influence our mindset. If we are surrounded by individuals who harbor limiting beliefs or discourage ambition, we may internalize these perspectives. Over time, this can create self-imposed limitations that hinder personal growth and achievement.

3. Stagnation:

Negative associations can contribute to a sense of stagnation. If the people around us are resistant to change or unwilling to pursue personal development, it can be challenging to break out of a cycle of complacency. Growth often requires a supportive environment that encourages exploration and continuous improvement.

Choosing Your Circle:

Given the powerful impact of association on our lives, it becomes imperative to be intentional about the company we keep. Choosing our circle of influence consciously can shape our journey toward success, fulfillment, and well-being.

1. Reflection and Assessment:

Take time to reflect on the people in your life and assess how they contribute to your overall well-being. Consider whether your associations align with your values, goals, and aspirations. This reflection is a crucial step in understanding the dynamics of your social connections.

2. Setting Boundaries:

Recognize the importance of setting boundaries in relationships. If certain associations consistently contribute negativity or hinder your progress, it may be necessary to establish healthy boundaries or, in some cases, reevaluate the extent of your engagement with those individuals.

3. Seeking Positive Influences:

Actively seek out positive influences that align with your goals. Attend networking events, join groups with shared interests, and engage with communities that foster growth and positivity. Surrounding yourself with individuals who inspire and uplift you creates a more conducive environment for personal development.

4. Continuous Learning:

Embrace a mindset of continuous learning and personal development. Engage with individuals who are knowledgeable in areas you aspire to grow in. This could involve seeking out mentors, attending workshops, or participating in communities focused on learning and growth.

5. Encouraging Mutual Growth:

Cultivate relationships that encourage mutual growth. Surround yourself with people who are not only supportive but also invested in their individual development. This creates a collective momentum towards positive change and success.

Impact on Personal and Professional Life:

The power of association extends to both personal and professional realms, influencing various aspects of our lives.

1. Career Success:

In the professional sphere, the people we associate with can impact our career trajectory. Positive professional relationships can open doors to opportunities, mentorship, and collaboration. On the other hand, negative associations may hinder career advancement and limit access to valuable networks.

2. Emotional Well-being:

Our emotional well-being is intricately connected to the quality of our relationships. Positive associations contribute to a supportive emotional environment, while negative associations can lead to stress, anxiety, and a diminished sense of self-worth.

3. Goal Achievement:

The pursuit of goals and aspirations is often a collaborative effort. Positive associations can provide the necessary encouragement, guidance, and resources to facilitate goal achievement. Conversely, negative associations may introduce obstacles and detract from the focus required to reach objectives.

4. Personal Fulfillment:

Ultimately, the power of association plays a crucial role in our overall sense of fulfillment. Meaningful connections, shared successes, and a supportive community contribute to a richer, more satisfying life. Choosing associations that align with your values and aspirations enhances the likelihood of experiencing personal fulfillment.

In essence, the power of association is a guiding force that shapes the trajectory of our lives. The individuals we surround ourselves with influence our mindset, attitudes, and behaviors, ultimately impacting the outcomes we experience. Being intentional about our social connections, recognizing the influence of positive and negative associations, and actively cultivating a circle that aligns with our values and goals are essential steps toward creating a life of purpose, positivity, and achievement. By harnessing the transformative potential of positive associations and mitigating the impact of negative influences, we empower ourselves to navigate life's journey with resilience, authenticity, and a greater capacity for success and fulfillment.

HABITS OF
THE SUCCESSFUL

In the relentless pursuit of making every year your year, understanding the specific habits that propel individuals into the top 1% becomes a guiding beacon. By assimilating these habits into your daily life, you can create a roadmap for your own journey to success.

The Power of Consistency

1. Daily Rituals and Routines

Consistency is not a one-time effort; it's a commitment woven into the fabric of daily life. Successful individuals start their days with purposeful morning rituals, setting a positive tone. This could range from meditation and goal visualization to a healthy breakfast that fuels both body and mind. Evening routines ensure restful sleep and reflection, preparing them for the challenges and opportunities of the next day.

2. Goal Setting and Achievement

Goal setting is a cornerstone habit of the successful. Beyond merely setting goals, they break them down into actionable steps. The process involves creating a roadmap, tracking progress, and celebrating milestones. This habit not only propels them forward but also ensures a sense of direction and purpose.

The Mindset of Success

1. Growth Mindset

A growth mindset is the fertile soil where success blossoms. Successful individuals view challenges as opportunities to learn and grow. They embrace setbacks as stepping stones, constantly seeking ways to improve. Cultivating a growth mindset involves reframing failures as lessons and maintaining an unwavering belief in one's capacity for improvement.

2. Positive Self-Talk and Visualization

The mind is a powerful force that can either propel or hinder success. Successful individuals engage in positive self-talk, silencing the inner critic and replacing negative thoughts with affirmations of capability and resilience. Visualization is a practice where they mentally rehearse success, reinforcing a positive expectation of the future. These habits create a mental environment conducive to achievement.

Time Management and Productivity

1. Prioritization and Time Blocking

Effectively managing time is a hallmark of successful individuals. They prioritize tasks, focusing on high-impact activities. Time blocking ensures dedicated periods for specific tasks, reducing multitasking and increasing overall efficiency. This habit not only enhances productivity but also ensures that energy is directed toward the most impactful endeavors.

2. Delegation and Outsourcing

Recognizing the value of delegation sets the most successful apart. They understand that focusing on their strengths and delegating tasks that others can handle more effectively is a strategic move. Outsourcing responsibilities, whether in personal or professional spheres, frees up time for strategic thinking and high-impact activities.

Networking and Relationship Building

1. Strategic Networking

Building a robust network is a habit that successful individuals prioritize. They attend networking events, engage on digital platforms, and nurture meaningful connections. This habit not only opens doors to new opportunities but also creates a support system of like-minded individuals.

2. Mentorship and Continuous Learning

Mentorship is a bridge to success. Successful individuals seek guidance from those with more experience, accelerating their learning curve. They are committed to continuous learning, staying abreast of industry trends, and acquiring new skills. This habit ensures that they are always evolving and adapting to this highly dynamic world.

Resilience and Adaptability

1. Embracing Challenges

Resilience is a trait forged through challenges. Successful individuals not only endure setbacks but thrive amidst adversity. They view challenges as opportunities for growth, learning, and innovation. Embracing challenges with a positive mindset is a habit that propels them forward, even in the face of uncertainty.

2. Adaptability in a Changing World

In a world marked by constant change, adaptability is a survival skill. Successful individuals not only accept change but embrace it as a force for innovation. They remain agile, open to new ideas, and quick to pivot when necessary. This habit ensures that they not only survive but thrive in a rapidly evolving landscape.

As you reflect on these habits of the successful, remember that they are not a distant blueprint but a set of principles you can incorporate into your own life. Begin by adopting one or two habits, and gradually integrating them into your routine. The journey to success is a marathon, not a sprint. Cultivate these habits, and in time, witness the transformative impact they can have on your path to making every year your year.

CONCLUSION

As we conclude this transformative journey through the pages of "How to Make Every Year Your Year," you've not only gained profound insights but have also taken the first steps toward shaping a successful future. The road to success is rarely walked alone, I am honored that you have invested time to learn how you could make every year your year.

My Team and I would like to invite you to join our community of High Performers which we call Total Freedom Nation.

I started sharing my journey on my Facebook and Instagram accounts with the sole purpose of transforming the lives of others just the way that I did. This fulfilling hobby quickly started to grow and became an income stream for our family.

We've partnered with one of the largest Health, and Fitness Brands in the World and have merged Health and nutrition, with High-Performance Development along with an income stream option. The foundation for building unshakable confidence is through health and fitness.

You will also need energy and stamina to go out in the world to create financial stability for you and the people who depend on you.

I felt, improve my wellness and get paid to help other people do the same.

It's definitely a win-win.

I learned that I have a passion for creating systems, teaching people better time management practices, developing leaders, and much more.

All because I followed my passion for health and fitness and turned that into a scalable business with other amazing like-minded individuals who are also out there creating thriving businesses and living high-performing lives that support their families.

Nothing makes me happier than seeing others succeed and reach their full potential. We are committed to becoming the best version of ourselves that we can be! I love my work and I am excited about the current opportunities and future ones to come.

First a foremost we are a Family and Family is EVERYTHING!! This is why our community of like-minded people is there to support you throughout this journey and beyond.

How can I best serve you?

We can work together in a few different ways. If you are looking to start your health journey or start your own business helping others do the same, you can learn more about our Business Mentorships here.

If you are a business owner seeking 1:1 mentorship, group coaching, or business consultations, we can help you here as well.

Make sure to follow me on Facebook and Instagram under Kenneth Barnes Jr. and Premier 1 Benefits to stay up to date on all my newest launches, motivational messages, and events!

Visit us today at TotalFreedomNation.com and we will see you on the other side.

All the best!

Kenneth Barnes

*Join us on the path to success, and together,
let's make the journey extraordinary!*

Do Not Go Yet; One Last Thing To Do

If you enjoyed this book or found it useful, I'd be very grateful if you'd post a short review on Amazon. Your support does make a difference, and I read all the reviews personally so I can get your feedback and make this book even better.

Thanks again for your support!